MARRIED BUT SINGLE

What Readers Are Saying About
Married But Single

" This is an excellent guide that you have created. I applaud you for getting it done. Marriage is definitely not a walk in the park. Chapter 8 was my favorite. No one else is responsible for our happiness. I really love that you wrote this. Congratulations again!" - Angela Hewlitt

"Upon reading your book, it mirrors what I'm going through, and I feel like the book understands what's happening in my life. I'm on lesson seven. The book feels like it speaks to women, when women question "why?" and [helps them] understand that they're not the only one feeling this way. It's a page turner! Remarkable. I'm doing the homework after each lesson. I love it. Congrats girl! "
- Amanda D.

Married But Single

A guide for wives who have considered leaving when love is not enough.

Charita D. Matthews

Unless otherwise indicated, all Scripture quotations are taken from the New King James Version of the Holy Bible. Scripture quotations marked (KJV) are taken from the King James Version of the Holy Bible.

© 2023 by Charita D. Matthews

Married But Single: A guide for wives who have considered leaving when love is not enough

The characters and events portrayed in this book are fictitious. Any similarity to real persons, living or dead, is coincidental and not intended by the author.

All rights reserved. No portions of this book may be reproduced, stored in a retrieval system, or transmitted in any form or by any means - electronic, mechanical, photocopy, recording, scanning, or other - except for brief quotations in critical reviews of articles, without the prior written permission of the publisher.

Atirah Media
Clinton, MD 20735
www.atirahmedia.com

Cover design by: Atirah Media
Printed in the United States of America

This guide is dedicated to all the women in my life who have given me the strength to become the woman and wife I am today.

To my maternal grandmother, Mother Elease P. Lorick. The epitome of the Proverbs 31 woman. An excellent wife. You laid the foundation for everything that I would become. Most of all, you showed me how to stand *and* serve alongside my husband. For 70 years, you never left my grandfather's side. Thank you for showing me how to love.

To my paternal grandmother, Mrs. Frances Pearson. You became a widow so early in life. Yet you managed to successfully raise 10 children. Your resilience and resourcefulness were something to be admired. Even the last time I saw you; you pressed a dollar and a piece of candy into my baby boy's hand. Your love and generosity will never be forgotten.

To my mother, Mrs. Geneva Lorick Pearson. You showed me how to have both strength and grace, a gentle and quiet spirit. This is not something that comes easy to me. Thank you for always being an example I can look to when I fall short.

To my Godmother, Mrs. Eloise Fairley. I understand exactly why you were chosen as my godmother. Even though we lived 500 miles apart I have your strong spirit, endurance, and heart for benevolence. I imagine my mother looking at me when I was born and seeing that fire in my eyes, the same fire you had within you. I will continue to carry the torch.

To my God-given aunt, Mrs. Rhonda Green. You have always been the aunt who is a little bit holy and a little bit hood. Standing in the gap; saying all the things my mother didn't have the words to say. Thank you for always having a listening ear, a word of encouragement, and a kick in the butt when I needed it.

To all married women who have ever felt like they are sick and tired of being sick and tired.
We see you. You are never alone. You will smile again.

MARRIED BUT SINGLE

FOREWORD

> *Then the Lord God made a woman from the rib he had taken out of the man, and he brought her to the man.*
> *The man said, "This is now bone of my bones and flesh of my flesh; she shall be called 'woman,' for she was taken out of man."*
> *That is why a man leaves his father and mother and is united to his wife, and they become one flesh.*
> (Genesis 2:22-24 NIV)

This was the first marriage, performed by God himself. This ceremony was simple: no attendants, and only the animals for an audience... so different from today. Today we often have all the *hoopla* involved with weddings, but many of the marriages don't last very long.

I remember when I got married on October 22, 1946. My husband and I had a simple ceremony with both our families in attendance, and a few friends. The reception was very modest, a country family meal: fried chicken, potato salad, collard greens, cornbread, and cake. I can't remember all the food; I was the nervous bride! We must also remember that this was in 1946, toward the end of The Great Depression. Things were very scarce, and food was government rationed. Our marriage ceremony may have been very simple, but our marriage lasted for 70 blessed years. SEVENTY YEARS, FOUR MONTHS, THREE WEEKS, AND ONE DAY! Then my beloved husband passed away into God's presence. We were blessed with a lasting marriage because we loved one another and had respect for each other.

Ladies, if you want your marriage to last, you first must remember who you are. God made you with special gifts and talents, unique to us as females. We are naturally gifted with the ability to nurture, and to care. Some of you ladies have left your gifts unopened. However, I admonish you to open the special gift of respect for your husband. God gave you this gift, so OPEN IT.

Here are a few "tidbits" that you can use for a lasting marriage:

1. Respect your husband.
Respect is one of the requirements given for a lasting marriage. This action soon turns into love, resulting in a lasting relationship between you and your husband. Your husband appreciates honor and respect, and you gain the benefits of a mutually happy and loving relationship.

" … and the wife see that she reverences her husband." (Ephesians 5:33b KJV)

2. Talk to one another. Communication is the key.
If something is bothering you that you know may perhaps harm your marriage, don't sleep on it, talk to your husband about it.

"Be ye angry, and sin not: let not the sun go down upon your wrath." (Ephesians 4:26 KJV)

3. Be honest with each other.
Keeping secrets can be a major force in destroying your marriage.

"Confess your faults one to another, and pray one for another, that ye may be healed. The effectual fervent prayer of a righteous man [woman] availeth much. (James 5:16 KJV)

4. Avoid arguments.
Be careful what you say, and how you say it when you are talking. Refrain from negative body language to convey what you are unwilling to say verbally with your words. Know when to hush. It takes two people to argue.

"And be ye kind one to another, tenderhearted, forgiving one another, even as God for Christ's sake hath forgiven you." (Ephesians 4:32 KJV)

Ladies, as we take a good look at ourselves, we can clearly see the magnificent handiwork of God. You are uniquely made with special gifts and talents. Many of us have put our gifts away, unopened; but I want to commend my granddaughter, Charita, for sharing her gifts with others by writing this book.

So, ladies, remember that you were made for the man, and you are "fearfully and wonderfully" made. (Psalms 139:14 KJV) Yes, we are GOD'S GEMS; his precious jewels! So, if you want to have a marriage that lasts, you must work at it. May you be blessed with many happy years of wedded bliss!

- Mother Elease P. Lorick

CHARITA D. MATTHEWS

Married But Single: A guide for wives who have considered leaving when love is not enough

TABLE OF CONTENTS

Introduction i
Preface iii

Lesson 1 | When you're wondering why Eve ate that apple .. 1

Lesson 2 | When there's more month than money 5

Lesson 3 | When you're not feeling the love 9

Lesson 4 | When you need a break 15

Lesson 5 | When you're not included 21

Lesson 6 | When the grass looks greener 27

Lesson 7 | When boys will be boys 31

Lesson 8 | When you think you can do bad all by yourself...39

Afterword 49
Wisdom from one wife to another 53
Reaffirming Your Love & Commitment to Marriage 55
Recommended books for further reading..................... 59

INTRODUCTION

For women who grew up in church (like me), we sometimes assume we have all the tools and resources needed to sustain the forever we were promised. The reality is marriage is a complex and many-splendored thing, for which there is not a one size fits all solution to every situation.

Married But Single is a guide to help women navigate the real-life situations that make you want to throw in the towel and file for divorce. Based on biblical foundations, this guide will outline practical ways to face many of the challenges a wife can find herself dealing with.

These lessons were compiled from real-life events I have personally experienced, as well as advice I have either shared or have been the recipient of over the years. It's more than a prayer and a bible verse. It is specific guidance that will help with processing the day-to-day thoughts and feelings you may experience as a wife. This guide can be used for self-reflection, book club discussions or for group classes.

CHARITA D. MATTHEWS

MARRIED BUT SINGLE

PREFACE

After thirteen years of marriage, I was ready to call it quits. Knowing all too well what was expected of me as a woman of faith, the heaviness of the relationship had taken its toll. Don't get me wrong, my husband is a great guy and an amazing dad. But carrying the burden of building a life together seemed to be too much, and forever sounded like a long time to feel this way.

At times I wondered, had I made a mistake? Did I miss the signs and red flags? My heart told me no. There were no red flags. If you knew our story, God had orchestrated things to bring us together at just the right time. We courted and went through all the protocols of doing things "the right way". Yet still, I found myself in this cycle of feeling frustrated, lonely, and incredibly sad.

Wherever you are and however you are feeling about your marriage, I can guarantee many wives have felt exactly the same as you do. This is not a means to belittle your experience, but rather to assure you that your feelings are both normal and valid. The worst part of going through a rough patch can be feeling as though no one understands what's happening to you.

One of the most important and memorable pieces of marriage advice is one that I received from the pastor who officiated my wedding, Pastor Tyrone Stevenson, PhD. He simply said to my husband and I, "never fall out of love at the same time."

At 24 years old, I had no context to help me understand what he meant. However, fourteen years of marriage has definitely put things into perspective. When I'm feeling low, my husband's love will hold me up. And in times when he's feeling low, my love will hold him up. My hope is that this guide will impart wisdom and clarity to help prevent wives from feeling hopeless.

MARRIED BUT SINGLE

LESSON 1

When you're wondering why Eve ate that apple

The book of Genesis outlines the story of the first marriage; the way our Creator originally intended it to be. In chapter 3, there's one line that has always stood out to me. It says, "Your desire shall be for your husband, and he shall rule over you." (Genesis 3:16 NKJV)

I've never really had anyone explain this passage to me. But it seems to be the very basis of marital conflict. The more I think about it, this passage seems to describe a power struggle. This first, perfect marriage was meant to be a harmonious union. Two humans, equal in power, having dominion over the earth and everything in it. However, Adam and Eve make a choice which introduces sin (along with its consequences) into the equation.

> The very next verse goes on to address Adam. It reads,
> *Then to Adam He said, "Because you have heeded the voice of your wife and have eaten from the tree of which I commanded you, saying, 'You shall not eat of it': "Cursed is the ground for your sake; In toil you shall eat of it all the days of your life.*
> (Genesis 3:17 NKJV)

My main takeaway from this passage is that mankind was not created to *toil*. For me, it's an easy explanation for why I always feel stressed. If you put these two pieces of the puzzle together in a present-day situation, imagine the following: Deep down in my soul I long to roam freely in paradise in the company of my loving husband; Stress-free and without conflict. Instead, I work all day just to turn around and manage the household all evening, then spend all my hard-earned money paying the bills. Even without conflict, that's enough to make anyone feel overwhelmed!

Life itself is all a balancing act. Sometimes, the addition of balancing a marriage creates the feeling that the whole thing is going to topple over and crash at your feet. What can prevent this feeling you ask? So many married couples have been asked this question and answered by saying, "communicate". In my opinion this is not entirely incorrect. It's an oversimplified pseudo-solution, often given with little to no additional guidance. So, let's unpack this a bit.

A huge part of effective communication is managing your own personal expectations. This goes a long way to minimize your emotional response to disappointment. As a young wife I found myself trying to make my husband live up to ideals that I had fantasized about as a child. Things that he was unaware of because these expectations lived only inside my head. They included relationships I saw in the movies and on tv, as well as couples in my life whose relationships had blossomed in a different place and time. I also often compared my husband to my father. My father is a hardworking baby boomer with ideals that are very similar, but slightly different than that of my husband.

I can recall a very specific example of what this looks like. In Maryland, it snows during the winter. Not a cute little dusting, but *SNOW* snow. All through my childhood, my father would salt the sidewalk and driveway the night before a heavy snow. Then in the morning, he would clear the snow off all the cars and shovel the porch, stairs, sidewalk & driveway before putting down a fresh layer of salt for traction.

For the first several years after I got married, I expected my husband to do the same things I saw my father do. I would get up for work with the expectation of walking out and getting into a clean car. The reality I soon came to realize, is that if snow was in the forecast, I should plan to get up earlier and clean my car off… I was extremely confused by this, but I didn't say anything. Instead, year after year I would have the same expectation, always keeping in mind I should be prepared to shovel my own way out. Eventually this random disappointment trickled into unrelated arguments. It was part of a laundry list of "ways my husband doesn't care about me".

The part I was overlooking was, my husband was completely unaware he was supposed to do these things. It seemed obvious to me a clear connection existed: snow falls; snow needs to be shoveled; a *good* husband would shovel the snow for his wife. It made sense to me as I'm sure it does for many others. But consider this; what if my husband's father didn't shovel snow? If my husband never saw anyone shovel snow, how would he know this is what it is expected of him? The fact is he did not make this connection. In his mind if the snow is safe enough to drive in, you clean your car off and go. If the snow is not safe enough to drive in, a wife should stay home until it is safe. To him, the obvious thing is that snow melts so it's no one's responsibility to shovel it. Which begs the question, who was wrong in this scenario?

As this example illustrates, several areas of miscommunication can exist all within one issue. Now imagine several issues and points of conflict happening all at once, on top of crying babies, annoying co-workers and everything else life tends to throw at us as wives. In this lesson, I want us to think about having realistic expectations, clearly communicating what those are, and leaving space for judgment-free trial and error as hubby makes the necessary adjustments to meet and exceed your expectations. This all is a process. But for two people committed to making it work, it's definitely possible.

Questions for reflection/discussion:

1. What unspoken expectations do you have for your spouse?
2. Are these expectations realistic or are they a fantasy?
3. In what ways are you prepared to compromise as you allow your husband space and time to adjust?

PERSONAL REFLECTION

LESSON 2

When there's more month than money

Many of us are familiar with the old adage, *opposites attract*. In many cases this plays out as a saver being attracted to a spender. I found this to be true for myself. It is so important for youth and young adults to learn how to manage their finances as early as possible. But if you haven't figured it out by the time you get married, is it too late?

In my opinion, it's never too late to take control of your personal finances. When merging a household however, these conversations can be nothing short of frustrating. The main issue being that individuals can have differing opinions on how to prioritize expenses.

Ponder this; if you need a phone to communicate, does that mean you should use a payment plan to get the newest phone when it's released every year? Personally, I would much rather put that extra money towards the increased energy bill that tends to occur during the winter months.

With that being said, if you're the spender in the marriage, it's important to consider how your purchases affect the family and think of ways you can get the same result without spending as much money. If there is no way to eliminate a specific expense, find ways to cut back on something else. For example, if you must take a vacation every year, then don't buy brand new outfits and shoes. You could visit a consignment shop instead of paying retail prices for clothing. Or you could very well wear what you already have in your closet.

Conversely, if you are the saver in the marriage, it may take some time for your spouse to adjust and stick to a tighter budget. In the meantime, you can manage things within your control and scale back as much as possible. For example, cut down the cable bill, downgrade your phone plan, take your lunch to work, coupon and/or co-op shop for groceries with family and friends.

During the first few years of our marriage, my husband and I decided not to install cable TV or a landline phone. Growing up everyone thought the internet bundle was definitely a necessary part of successfully adulting. However, I became an early adopter of what was known as a cord cutter. We invested in a basic internet plan and opted for a streaming service which was free at the time. Although we now have two subscription services as opposed to the one free service we started out with, this was a very simple way to reduce expenses as we adjusted to merging our finances.

If you really find yourself struggling from month to month, don't be ashamed to ask for help. The first year or two after becoming a mom, I was on WIC (public assistance for women, infants, and children). The way I saw things, I had been working and paying into the system since I was 15 years old. Therefore, I was basically using my own money and had nothing to be ashamed about. Also, ask family and friends for help. You'd be surprised to find aunts, uncles and grandparents are eager and willing to help if you need assistance with things such as gas, food, baby items or school supplies. You won't know if you don't ask.

Dealing with finances can really make or break a marriage, especially in the early stages. In the midst of things, you may feel you want to scream and pull your hair out. But in the end, having these conversations will be worth it.

Questions for reflection/discussion:

1. What beliefs or routines regarding finances did you bring into your marriage from your childhood or single life?
2. For the spenders: What can you cut back on to help save money for the family?
3. For the savers: Have you shared the household budget with your spouse? This can be an eye-opening experience for those who have never maintained a budget for personal expenses.

PERSONAL REFLECTION

_____

_____

_____

LESSON 3

When you're not feeling the love

I'm all for the advancement of women and female empowerment. But I personally have no interest in bringing home the bacon <u>*and*</u> frying it up in a pan. I have to laugh at the phrase because, whose idea was this? Contributing to the household in various ways is extremely important in order to support a healthy and balanced family environment. More important than that, however, is dividing responsibilities in a way that makes sense; TO YOU.

The division of household labor has changed so much over the years. In my opinion, society's expectations are lagging far behind. For me personally, this became a point of dissension that affected my marriage in many ways. Generally, the problem was I didn't have enough hours in the day. In this day and age, women are expected to work a full-time job, get advanced degrees, run a side hustle, drive the minivan to soccer practice, prepare homemade meals, keep the house spotless, workout, meditate, check the kids' homework, visit friends & family, go to church, feed the homeless, save the whole world and still be ready to *take care of her wifely duties*. It's enough pressure to make anyone lose their mind. And trust me, I almost did.

Spending eight or more hours at work, and two hours commuting was already a challenge. Then I had a baby and decided to take a step back from everything else I was involved in so I could complete my bachelor's degree. During this period of time, so many people stepped up to help me manage everything because I was a new mom. When I tell you they stepped up, people cooked meals for my family, cleaned my house and watched my son without me having to ask or pay. After I graduated and my son got a little older, the responsibilities kept piling on. The only difference is now I should be able to manage everything on my own... Right?

In many ways, that's a reasonable expectation. But in actuality, if you approached any random wife and mom on the street you might be surprised to find she's completely overwhelmed with trying to balance her responsibilities. This includes everyone's schedules, finances, daily household tasks and her personal development which is an important part of how a woman measures her value in the world. Ironically, I was doing all these things and on the outside, it looked amazing. Quite often people would ask me how I was able to be so efficient and organized. And I had answers; Jesus, coffee, and Google! What I really should have been telling women (which I do now) is to put some of that stuff down. Maybe even all of it.

During the COVID shut down, when I tell you I put EVERYTHING down, you could not convince me to do anything extra. Not a prayer call, not a PTA meeting... *Nothing*. That period of time was such an eye-opening experience that forced me to re-evaluate the way I looked at things I had involved myself in. In hindsight, my sanity had been hanging on by a thread. My husband works long, unpredictable hours so I didn't directly blame him for my being overwhelmed. But there were definitely times when I became frustrated with my situation. That's when the LONG list of receipts came out. The days when the bills weren't paid, the nights when I felt lonely. Those times when I wanted to go to grad school or start a business, but who was going to watch the baby? How about the stress of constantly having to figure out what's for dinner every night for eternity? I found that although these things were expected of me, I wasn't built for it. Luckily, I don't have to live up to anyone's expectations. Isn't that great? Coming to that realization was definitely a freeing experience for me. And let me tell you, with the support of a few friends and a great therapist, I began to rebuild my life in a way that was more practical and realistic in ways that were important to me.

This all started as a conversation with my husband. I let him know I was exhausted and overwhelmed. Then I explained what things in my environment were contributing to the way I felt. Being clear about which aspects I had control over and which ones I did not was an important piece of the puzzle. But focusing on solutions is what kept this discussion from turning into an argument. We spoke in detail about what tasks he could take on that would help me breathe a bit easier. Some things had a simple solution. For example, I asked why he kept forgetting to take out the trash. I was a bit amused to find he didn't have a reason. It's common to prioritize other tasks, become busy and forget. That's understandable. In return he asked me a question; why isn't this 8-year-old child of ours taking out the trash? As crazy as it sounds, the thought never occurred to me that my precious baby boy should be taking out the trash. But guess what, he started taking the trash out that very week.

Other tasks such as laundry and cutting the grass we decided to hire out, either because nobody wanted to do it or because the task wasn't being completed consistently. The goal in all of this was to create balance and peace of mind. Now this conversation was one that I had to be vulnerable and transparent for. Had my husband not been receptive to my approach, I would have found another way before ultimately handling this on my own. Not in a petty way as I am certainly capable of; but in the sense that he didn't care *how* things got done as long as they were done. I chose to involve him in the conversation so he would understand I'm not superwoman and I'm no longer trying to be. This was a moment where I had to advocate on my own behalf for the greater good of the family. Because if I didn't speak up, then who the heck would?

I want to stress the importance of being clear on what love and support look like for you. In recent years, there has been a lot of focus on what astrological sign you are and what your love language is in terms of how people should love you. Those are good places to start, but there are so many different ways to express love and support that you cannot put a label on. The best way to help your husband figure out what this looks like is to take off the superwoman mask and cape. Give him a chance to love the *real* you.

Questions for reflection/discussion:

1. Make a list of all your responsibilities and commitments outside of home and work.
   a. Reflect on why you got involved.
   b. Evaluate if you're still making an impact.
   c. Determine if you need to be in a leadership role vs a support/advisor position.
2. What are some household tasks you could delegate to your child(ren) or hire out?
3. What activities or organizations are you involved in that re-energize you when you're feeling stressed or overwhelmed? If you don't have any, make a short list of options.

PERSONAL REFLECTION

_____

_____

_____

LESSON 4

When you need a break

I'm going to address the elephant in the room... Wouldn't this all be much easier if you could just leave? I'd be lying if I said I never had these thoughts. If I left, I might be distracted for a while with all the tasks that go along with the process of uncoupling. But after it's all said and done, all I really would have accomplished is running away from my problems.

During times when you feel as though you need a break, there are certainly ways to do that and work on your marriage at the same time. Over the years I have become a fan of staycations, meaning I would take a vacation while in my home, or extremely close to home. While on my staycation, sometimes I would book a hotel an hour or so away from my home as a means to clear my head without all the responsibilities of being a wife and a mom. I could sleep without someone calling my name, eat without someone asking for a bite and shower without anyone poking their head around the curtain. You'd be surprised by how much easier it is to deal with managing a home after taking a break. Other times, when money was tight, I would opt to stay with a friend or at my parents' house. As long as I had some quality alone time, I could return to my own home feeling refreshed.

If you feel like you need space to figure things out, staycations can help, but I would also suggest seeking the support of a counselor or therapist. Personally, I have support from a whole team of mental health specialists. First, my husband and I have a counselor for marriage *and* individual counseling. She knows all of my super personal business as well as the nuances of my marriage. Then I have a licensed clinical therapist. She is my therapist alone and in terms of resolving conflict, her loyalty lies with me. Finally, I had the pleasure of working with an amazing confidence coach. In the beginning I partnered with her for business reasons, but the work we did trickled over into all areas of my life. This may sound like a lot, but all of these things were needed. Especially in times when I felt like I had lost myself. Having gotten married at 24 years old and becoming a mom at 27, it's equally possible I never knew who I truly was to begin with.

What we're really talking about here is self-care which is defined as, "the practice of taking an active role in protecting one's own well-being and happiness, in particular during periods of stress." (Oxford Languages) Self-care practices can vary depending upon each person and the situation they may be dealing with. However, sometimes the same person can try more than one approach to address the same situation.

In my home, I often deal with clutter. The clutter is everywhere, in every room and the clutter persists no matter how much I try to prevent it. There was a period of time when I ignored it because I was overwhelmed in other areas of life. I lacked the mental and physical capacity to reduce or eliminate the clutter. There were other times when I compulsively tried to eliminate it. Walking into a cluttered home negatively affected my mood on a daily basis, so I tried a few things to improve the situation. First, I threw everything away. And by everything, I mean almost anything that wasn't literally nailed down. Next, I rearranged the furniture to create a more open and airy space where I could think and breathe. Then, I added shelving and storage bins for my family to organize various items rather than cluttering the common spaces in our home. But no matter what I did, the clutter just kept coming back.

Ultimately, I used a combination of these tactics to address the issue. First and foremost, I hold my family responsible for re-homing their personal items. Also, I'm still proactively providing storage solutions to minimize the overall impact of the clutter. When I have the capacity to deep clean, I do. But when I'm too overwhelmed, I find other ways to create a space where I can decompress or release anxiety. In most cases this includes fresh air and being near water. Spending time in nature has a grounding affect for me. A simple walk near the lake in our local park does wonders. It allows me to refresh myself and reset my mood.

Finding what works for you may involve a period of trial and error. Beginning with evaluating your workday and external commitments, finding time for self-care may even require setting some boundaries in order to support your needs. Also, starting small can be helpful if you are new to including self-care in your routine. Even ten to fifteen minutes of quiet time can make a huge impact if you've been getting zero personal time thus far. Also, self-care is not just for moms. Wives with grown children or no children deserve quiet time as well. This is not something you have to earn. It's also important to note, everyone in the home needs their own personal quiet time especially at the end of a workday or school day. Carrying the stress of the day into the home and then making an attempt to communicate and interact with each other can be a recipe for disaster. Finding healthy ways to take a break is so important and will have a lasting impact on the atmosphere in your home.

Before you consider leaving your marriage, do the hard work of setting aside time to reflect and identify what the underlying issues really are. Not the surface stuff, but the deep roots which are the essence of who we are and why we do certain things. You might be surprised to find all your issues are "figureoutable". That isn't a real word but trust me, it's totally a thing.

Questions for reflection/discussion:

1. Make a short list of budget friendly places you could visit as a staycation for a few days.
2. Take some time to reflect on the things that are causing conflict or making you unhappy. When you peel back the layers, what are the underlying issues?
3. Using pen and paper, write a letter to your spouse outlining what these underlying issues are. Include what you are willing to do to resolve them. Throw the letter away and write a second draft. This practice will help you become clearer in how you communicate before you approach the conversation with your husband.

PERSONAL REFLECTION

LESSON 5

When you're not included

Have you ever felt left out? As if you weren't a part of your marriage, but were instead just a roommate? I sure have. My husband is an entrepreneur which I was aware of while we were dating. It was something I admired about him, as he had started his first business when he was still in high school.

However, two years into our marriage, we made the decision that he would become a full-time entrepreneur. That in essence was the long and short of my involvement in the process. Although we had the same goals, the idea of what the process would look like was very different for each of us. As I said, he started his first business in the 11th grade. He was very independent at a young age. While he has always had strong leadership and motivational skills, he never learned how to effectively partner with someone. There were so many times business decisions were made independently which negatively impacted our family, such as financial investments and committing to contracts with evening and overnight hours. Many times, these decisions were made without even so much as a heads up prior to him leaving for a shift.

Initially, I took this personally. However, as time went on, I realized he wasn't even making the connection between what he was doing and how I felt about it. In his mind the goal was to take care of the family. As far as he was concerned, so long as the family was safe, and the bills were paid he was fulfilling his duty as a husband. I can own up to having brought my concerns to him in a less than constructive manner, which of course didn't turn out the way I'd hoped. Thankfully, couple's counseling helped a lot with learning how to communicate effectively and form a partnership. In counseling we considered our personality styles and how that impacts how we relate to each other.

My husband is very extroverted. He's a people person which makes sense considering the way he conducts business. He loves networking and collaborating with people in order to find solutions to problems. For this reason, he gets lost in his work and doesn't even realize how much time he's spending outside the home. Me on the other hand, being an introvert, I got married so I wouldn't have to talk to anyone else besides my spouse. I'm just kidding, but in all honestly my day begins winding down around 6pm. I work in customer service. Ironically the same collaboration and problem solving that energizes and excites my husband is draining to me. After my workday ends, I go home to care for our son and manage the household until bedtime. By the time my husband gets home expecting to spend time together, I'm asleep. Although we each had expectations around how our relationship would look on a daily basis, we had to figure out what was realistic based on our individual needs. Our communication now is far from perfect but it's MUCH better than it was in the early years of our marriage.

That was my very personal experience of having my husband's business take precedence. What if your husband doesn't run a business, but still is not operating as a unit?

There are many transitions that take place when two adults decide to join together as one. It's not a magical thing that occurs when you say, "I do". For many, part of that transition is dealing with a spouse who still wants to hang out with his friends. Although you are building a life together, your individual interests don't disappear into thin air. Even as a wife, there are some things you have to re-prioritize, such as hobbies. In the same manner, your husband may not realize where these adjustments need to occur. Better yet, he may be convinced that he has made the necessary adjustments. For example, maybe he comes home at 10 p.m. instead of midnight as he did when he was single. That's a good thing, right? But what if in this same example, the wife expects him to be home right after work to help with the kids? This is a huge miscommunication that can lead to arguments and resentment if it's not addressed early on.

There are a few strategies I found to be helpful in situations where expectations do not meet reality. The first thing is to state what you want. Men are not mind readers; you have to talk about what it is you want and sometimes include the *why*. Communicating your why can remove the aspect of an ask being perceived as nagging. You're not complaining about the issue for no reason, you're expressing a concern for the greater good of the household.

Another way to address this type of issue is to connect with other married couples. It's okay to have single friends. But if all of your friends are single, they may be inadvertently causing you to cross boundaries simply because they don't share similar responsibilities. If finding couples to hang out with is difficult, consider making a safe space for the guys to hang out at your house. After all it's not the fact that he's spending time with others that's the problem. The issue is the lack of support at home. If the guys are hanging out at your house, you get the best of both worlds. Hubby is home to give a helping hand when needed, and the kids get to see their "uncles" who will likely distract the kids for a little while and give you a break.

That is just one example of how to find a middle ground where both you and your spouse's needs are met. It doesn't have to be all or nothing and the solution can be something completely different from what you initially suggested. The key to success is keeping an open mind.

Questions for reflection/discussion:

1. If you're frustrated about feeling left out, reflect on how this situation may have changed since you first got married. Was it always an issue, or has something changed that was not discussed?
2. Think about what level of support you need and what it looks like. Be prepared to share realistic examples of what would help you feel more included.
3. Maintaining your individuality is an important part of a successful forever. If you find it necessary to compromise, think about which hobbies and activities you both will be able to do separately and together without a major impact on balance. For example, schedule a bi-weekly date night together, but hubby hangs out on Friday nights while you enjoy a self-care Saturday to yourself. Remember, it's all about balance.

PERSONAL REFLECTION

_____

_____

_____

LESSON 6

When the grass looks greener

The year 2018 was the single most challenging year of my marriage thus far. It was a year during which I questioned everything. Was I good enough? Had I chosen the wrong spouse? What had I done wrong to cause my marriage to fail?

During this same year, I started a new job. Ironically, the colleague I ended up working alongside was in the beginning stages of a budding romance. Her beau wooed her as I watched; sending flowers, bringing her lunch, calling throughout the day to let her know he was thinking about her.

In my brokenness I envied her. Was I not deserving of all these same things? After months of intense marriage counseling, my husband and I were able to work through our issues and begin to rebuild our marriage.

Eventually, my coworker connected with me and shared a bit of her story. Both she and her friend had past relationships where they each faced a considerable amount of difficulty. The more she shared with me, the more I realized, what I was watching was the result of wisdom gained through trial and error. They were older and had been through situations which helped them recognize a good thing. Also, they were each willing to take the necessary steps to nurture the relationship.

What I was witnessing was the type of growth and maturity I aspired to. I'm so glad my colleague shared her story with me. The reality is, from the outside looking in you never know what that person or couple has been through to get where they are today. On the flip side of things, you also don't know if things are really as they seem. I'm certain there are other couples I've admired from afar, observing what was happening in public but not knowing they were living through hell behind closed doors. Be careful what you wish for…

In a previous chapter, I mentioned love languages. A series of books written by Gary Chapman introduces these concepts and their implications. My husband and I became of aware of and read this book very early in the courting phase of our relationship. We were literally teenagers; I was 18 and he was 19. Although we've always been aware of each other's love languages, it took a while to recognize the ebbs & flows and also the fact that most people are bi-lingual!

The bible says, "…Rejoice in the wife of your youth" (Proverbs 5:18) Rejoice simply means to show joy. This is an act or gesture toward your spouse in order to show affection and desire. Many of those who have looked outside their marriage did so because they didn't feel wanted or desired in the ways that were meaningful to them. In response, they failed to show joy toward their spouse, and as a result, the marriage began to wither away like un-watered grass.

So often we make the mistake of assuming others desire to feel love in the same ways we do. In my case, that would mean assuming everyone likes and prefers spending quality time together. My primary love language is quality time meaning I need you to hang out with me in order to feel loved. You don't have to bring anything and in most cases we don't even need to have plans. Simply carving out time in your day to occupy the same space as me, makes me feel loved.

Conversely, the way I show love to others is different from the way I prefer to receive it. Although I desire quality time, my first instinct in showing love to others is through acts of service. Meaning if you're ill or feeling down, I'm the friend who will show up and cook dinner for your kids or do your laundry, so you have the space you need in order to heal.

Keeping all of this in mind, it's important to consider your spouse may be desperately trying to show you love in the only way they know how. However, they may very well be speaking a language that is foreign to you. In my opinion, marriage counseling is akin to hiring a translator who helps each person understand what the other is trying to say or communicate. Counseling can be a great tool to help demystify minor misunderstandings and miscommunications that can snowball into larger issues. Take a closer look at your marriage. Then look at it from farther away. Sometimes the solution to your frustrations is simply a change of perspective.

Questions for reflection/discussion:

1. Comparison is the thief of all joy. Make a list of things you admire about your own marriage. Use this list to help combat envy and hold your negative thoughts captive.
2. Did you know your love language can change over time? Check in with your spouse to make sure the thoughtful gestures you both make toward each other are being received in the way they were intended.
3. Be honest, do you have a work boo or someone you fantasize about being with instead of your spouse? Take a moment to repent. Then create an affirmation statement to recite when those thoughts come to mind.

PERSONAL REFLECTION

_____

_____

_____

LESSON 7

When boys will be boys

There is so much to be said about infidelity. From the ways in which marriage and relationships were affected during slavery, to the ways mass incarceration plays a role, and everything in between. Many various socioeconomic, psychological, and physiological factors contribute to why infidelity has become so common, *especially* within the black community. While I know and understand all of these things, I still firmly believe there is no place for extramarital affairs. The same way I learned about all the things I mentioned, there is a vast amount of information readily available which can help men combat and overcome these urges. At the end of the day, each person has to want to do better.

With all of that said, where a true, medically diagnosed issue exists, these behaviors can change with a network of support. The same is true for those who experienced a family dynamic where extramarital affairs were normalized. What burdens me though, is an empty promise of change with no actions to go along with it. This can easily become a cycle of emotional abuse that often leaves a woman drained in many ways. In this chapter, I want to speak directly to women who are stuck in this type of cycle.

First of all, infidelity is a choice. Every marriage will experience ups and downs; no marriage is perfect. As a wife, nothing you did or said or failed to do is the reason why a choice was made to step outside the marriage. It's fine to explore ways to improve communication and intimacy. But your focus should not be to *keep him* from cheating. You could do anything he asks and everything you could think of. If he wants to step out anyway, he will. The responsibility of that choice lies only with the person making it.

Secondly, you are the only person who can make decisions about your marriage. Not your parents, not your siblings, not your friends, coworkers, pastor, or therapist. Although support and advice are beneficial, the choice you are faced with is one that you have to deal with the consequences of. Whatever that looks like. For me, anytime I considered divorce I thought about what my life would look like if I left my marriage. Where would I live, how would I pay bills, how would this affect my son? But I also considered what things would look like if I stayed. Would things ever get better? If they don't, is that something I can manage for the next 50-60 years? Think about it. Your vows state "for better or worse, for richer or poorer, in sickness and health, till death us do part." In small ways I was experiencing almost all of the difficult parts… at the same time. With life expectancy being upwards of 80 years old I just couldn't see myself doing that for the foreseeable future.

One of the most influential and powerful things I had a friend say to me during this time was, "whatever you choose, I support you and I'm here if you need anything." She understood and respected the weight of my decision. Also, she understood that injecting her opinion into the equation would only add an additional burden. If you make the choice to work on your marriage, which at the time I did, there are two things you need to keep in mind. First, never let anyone's opinion get in the way. Opinions are like butt holes; everybody has one. But no one is living your life or walking in your shoes. Only you are truly aware of what you can handle and what you cannot. Secondly, this may sound crazy... If you choose to stay in the marriage, don't stay in hopes that your husband will change. Stay in spite of what is going on. Your focus is not to change him; you are incapable of changing him and you have zero control over anything he is doing. Your goal is to honor your vows and work on YOU. Because guess what? No matter what you choose, you have to unpack and process all of the emotional fallout.

That in a nutshell is why I chose to stay and process my situation. This was a very personal choice. For me it was easier to stay and focus only on my emotional work than it would have been to simultaneously go through the process of uncoupling, finding a place to live, and working out living arrangements for our son. When I say stay and process, I don't mean be strong or get through it. Sometimes staying in order to process means allowing yourself to be vulnerable, to break down; to really *experience* what it is that you're going through. In order to grow through something, you have to go through it. I mentioned a friend who told me she supports my decision either way. During the times when I was on the floor crying, she was right there with me. Not picking me up, not telling me to be strong, or things will get better. At the time, she didn't know if things would get better or not. But she would lay on the floor with me, in silence and just *be with me* to support me and hold space. That's the kind of people you want around you. Not the ones who are telling you what you should or should not do. You want people who are going to help you process things in your own way and in your own time. That is how you heal from hurt.

So, what happens when you've tried everything, and you feel like giving up? One of my pet peeves is the *let go and let God* culture. Ironically, that's exactly what I'm about to tell you. But there's a difference in saying what to do and explaining how to do it. I'm going to illustrate my next point. Imagine your husband is stonewalling you, completely refusing to talk. This goes on for years no matter what you do or say. All you're met with is silence on the other end. The truth of the matter is you can't make a person talk to you. Not only that, in this scenario your husband is acting this way in order to trigger a response. If you keep reacting, the behavior will continue. You have to stop focusing on the person and try something different in order to get a different result.

Depending on your personality and temperament, this can be easier said than done. But if my husband decided he didn't want to talk to me I would take a moment to self-reflect on the way I'm contributing to the issue, then I would change my own behaviors in an effort to move forward. For me it's too difficult to try and function within the chaos. I get burned out easily and won't be able to manage my day-to-day life. So, I'm inclined to keep doing whatever it is I need to do. Not in a spiteful way, but in a productive manner which is focused on results. Regardless of what is happening between my husband and I, I still have a household to maintain, I'm still raising a son, I still have to get up and go to work every morning. Also,

I'm going to continue doing the things I committed to doing as a wife. If I was cooking, I would continue cooking; if I was cleaning, I'd keep cleaning. But life goes on. Once you process your emotions you have to find ways to move forward as opposed to getting stuck in this cycle of frustration. As the saying goes, what you feed grows. Stop feeding into a dysfunctional cycle. Allow yourself to break free from it.

In doing some personal work with my therapist, I was able to identify and take ownership of a cycle of my own. I suffer from seasonal depression. When it's warm and sunny outside my marriage is ok. Not perfect, but manageable. However, when the days grow shorter and it starts getting cold outside, all the little irritations and idiosyncrasies start to become more noticeable. Even though these issues always exist, as my mood begins to become melancholy, it's more difficult for me to manage my reaction to the things that bother me. Of course, I naturally started to turn my focus on everything and everyone else instead of looking within. Now that I'm aware of the cycle, I can get ahead of it. I actively communicate about things that bother me in the moment. That way there's no time for the issue to grow and fester. Also, when I notice the weather changing, I begin to incorporate more self-care into my routine in order to stabilize my mood. These are all things that help me communicate effectively.

When I first started using these techniques, my husband was still stuck in the previous cycles. It took some time for him to recognize the shift in my approach and then find his own way to adjust. Had he chosen to remain in the dysfunctional cycle, he would have just been there arguing with himself. Also, there wouldn't have been anything I could do to change his perspective had he been unwilling to adapt.

In closing this chapter, I want you to really be mindful of behaviors. Both your behaviors and those of your husband. Each action has a reaction. You both have to be aware of and take accountability for your own individual actions. These are important steps in the healing process. Also, if both parties agree to move forward and repair the marriage, each person has to look within and be honest about what they are willing to change and/or accept. Neither person can do the work for or carry the load of the other. And if you pretend to do the work, the same issue will continue to show up. You have to do the work.

Questions for reflection/discussion:

1. What patterns or cycles have you observed in your marriage?
2. After identifying the cycles, think about some possible triggers. When do the behaviors start? What could be causing these behaviors?
3. Talk about your reflections with your husband and include the support of a counselor or therapist if possible.

PERSONAL REFLECTION

_____

_____

_____

LESSON 8

When you think you can do bad all by yourself

If you've reached this chapter, the final chapter of the book, and you're sitting here realizing you see yourself in each one. If you're frustrated and wondering why you're even still in this marriage, I understand. I've been exactly where you are.

I was raised with the expectation of being a productive adult who makes meaningful contributions to society. A Godly wife who leaves & cleaves and is "fruitful". As an ambitious young adult, I entered the world and proceeded to check all the appropriate boxes in turn, Graduate college, check. Get a *good* job, check. Get married, check. Buy a house, check. Have a kid, check. I did all the things I was *supposed* to do. And nothing was detrimentally wrong, but my life looked completely different from what I thought it would. My marriage was trash, I felt like a failure as a parent, and I was completely hopeless as to how I could possibly turn things around.

From a young age I read all the books and took all the classes on relationships, communication, love & marriage, and respect & submission. Even after gleaning all that knowledge from various sources, I felt ill-equipped to fix my broken marriage. The truth is, I was. In essence I had all the tools in my toolbox. I even had the blueprint and a clear illustration of the goal in mind. The problem is, I was using everything incorrectly. In case you haven't noticed, this guide is not about how you can fix your marriage. Instead, each chapter has focused on how you as a woman can begin to move forward by embracing the season you're in and performing at the top of your role. What does that mean? It's a term that I borrowed from my corporate life.

While I'm at work, I'm not expected to do my supervisor's job. My position comes with outlined roles and responsibilities. If I desire to increase my value or fulfillment within the role, I don't create a situation where I'm in competition with my supervisor. Instead, I partner with them to find ways in which I can expand my duties so that the work I perform is more valuable for the team and more meaningful for me.

Likewise, as a wife it is not my role to lead the household. Nor is it my responsibility to swoop in and fix everything that's broken. My God-given task as a wife is to be a helpmeet. So instead of stressing over imperfect areas in my marriage, I begin with self-reflection. In what ways did I contribute to this issue? How am I out of alignment by trying to take the lead? Was I passive or active in the offense which allowed this issue to fester? Did I ignore a red flag in hopes the problem would resolve on its own?

Wherever I fall short, I take ownership and voice my concerns. Although we may or may not come to an agreement at that moment, I have communicated my expectations. From then on, I move differently in alignment with what was discussed. In the meantime, even if my husband continues on with business as usual, I operate at the top of my role. Being an example of what I expect while also staying in my lane gives my husband an opportunity to step up to the plate. As frustrating as it may seem, overstepping will get you the opposite result of what you're trying to accomplish.

In my own marriage, one of the biggest points of contention was the vast amount of time I spent alone. My husband is an entrepreneur, which I was aware of during the dating and engagement phases of our relationship. But as a wife, I struggled because the man works ALL THE TIME. It's not that I wanted to go out (although I wouldn't mind going out), but one of the reasons I got married was for companionship. I wasn't getting any of that; sis was in the house…

So, I asked, and I waited. Then I fussed, and I waited. Next, I was disappointed, and I continued to wait. Until I finally got sick of waiting. I became completely frustrated with feeling like I was the absolute last on his list of things to do. Even worse, I felt like he would never get the point no matter how many times I brought this to his attention. Thankfully, we sought counseling, and my therapist offered another perspective. Why had I decided my only option was to wait?

My husband was in a season of building which is still the case as I'm currently writing this guide. His focus as the leader of our household is firmly on providing for his family. Although he can observe that I'm lonely and frustrated, he doesn't see the immediate benefit of *chilling* when there's an opportunity to make money. In his eyes, if everything works out then we'll have a lifetime to chill, travel and watch the sunset together. Therefore, I can wait to enjoy the tradeoff of his efforts. My therapist helped me see that neither of us was *wrong*, which was fine for what it was. But in the meantime, *ion't wanna sit in the house no more*.

Thank God for an amazing therapist because she asked me a very simple question, "What is keeping me from going out?" Now part of this was challenging my nature as an introvert. Aside from that, what was keeping me lonely besides myself? Once I realized it was me, I started dating everyone. I take my son out to eat and to the movies. My mom and I go to conferences and attend plays together. Each of my friends share various interests with me; I now call them anytime I find a concert or restaurant I think they might enjoy. I even vacation with friends and extended family from time to time. After doing this for a while, I gained the confidence to take myself out on dates. I love it here. Instead of owning my responsibility to find joy, I had placed that role on my husband. But no one can love me the way I do. My husband is not supposed to BE my sole source of happiness and fulfillment, he is supposed to add to it in a healthy and balanced way.

The divine order is God first, self & family second, then career, vocation, etc. I was placing all my personal value and self-worth on how much attention I received from my spouse. In essence I had placed my marriage on the throne in place of God and that was where my attention was. That was a recipe for disaster from the start. The real solution is to connect with God and pour into yourself. Every other area of your life will collect the overflow.

I know one thing for certain and two things for sure, your life will never go 100% as you plan. But if you focus on yourself and stop trying to control every possible variable, I PROMISE you will find peace. Maybe not all day every day. As long as you're living and breathing you will continue to experience highs and lows. But you can find a bit of joy in every day if you look for it. Life is not supposed to fit into the perfect mold you created. The power is in releasing the illusion of control. You were never in control anyway… What you thought was control was actually you manipulating circumstances in a way that fit your preferences. I can tell you for a fact, there was a time when if even one thing fell out of place, my whole world came tumbling down along with my sanity. Let it go sis. Break the mold. Stop being a prisoner of circumstance.

Put your hope and trust in God. Focus on the things that you know to be true. I love my child and I'm not perfect, but I'm his favorite mom. I'm doing the best I can with what I have, and I get a little better at it with each passing day. Maybe today sucked, but I've survived 100% of my worst days. In some cases, I even learned something from the experience. I'm not telling you to hope for an uncertain future, I'm telling you to fully embrace and live in the present. That includes letting go of whatever it is you think you lost be it time, love, or whatever. You haven't lost anything or wasted time. You're winning with the hand you were dealt. As the bible says, "And we know that God causes all things to work together for good to those who love God, to those who are called according to His purpose." (Romans 8:28, NIV) Keep your head held high and walk confidently in your purpose as a wife and woman of God. You've got this sis.

Questions for reflection/discussion:

1. What are some things you can change to reduce your level of responsibility?
2. Where can you increase your efforts to make the most impact while staying in your lane?
3. What are some things you used to enjoy as a single woman that you can still enjoy alone while protecting the covenant of marriage?

PERSONAL REFLECTION

_____

_____

_____

MARRIED BUT SINGLE

NOTES

NOTES

AFTERWORD

The main reason for writing this guide was to give hope to wives who feel hopeless. I've had moments where I felt trapped and couldn't see a way out. Times when I envisioned an eternity of being stuck in an endless cycle of asking, "Where do we go from here?" I entitled this guide *Married But Single* because in so many ways I felt alone in my marriage. As if I were still single, left to fend for myself out here in these streets.

As a wife I desired protection, provision, and companionship; a mental, physical and spiritual covering. The most frustrating thing for me was having done everything by the book and not getting the expected result. I could have easily thrown the marriage away to find my forever husband. But without facing the root cause of the issues, I would have simply carried those conflicts right into the next relationship.

Ladies, this is not a quick & dirty guide to *pray and stay*. For me the '*stay*' part made me feel as though I was going to lose my mind. But I'm not a quitter; before I considered leaving, I had to be sure I gave the marriage everything I had.

If you're finding yourself in a similar situation, I hope this guide helped to uncover areas where you can challenge yourself to grow. Marriage is a mirror which stirs up thoughts and feelings you either tried to avoid or didn't know were there. Wherever life and marriage take you, there are always growth opportunities. Allow these lessons to lead you on a path that preserves your mental and emotional well-being.

MARRIED BUT SINGLE

WISDOM FROM ONE WIFE TO ANOTHER

I posed the following question to my inner circle of sister-friends:
> *"If you could give wives from all walks of life any one piece of advice for a successful marriage, what would it be? The caveat is, you cannot say "communicate" or "Keep God first".*

"You will have good days and bad days. Sometimes you may not like your spouse but that has nothing to do with love. Neither one of you is perfect, so accept the faults and move on. But know that prayer and counseling always help. Talk your differences out with somebody!"
- Mrs. Geneva L. Pearson married since 1980

"The key to a successful marriage is acknowledging there is no perfect marriage. Both should equally give 100%. Practice patience and always give [your husband] a hug each morning."
- Mrs. Mikema Defang, married since 2013

"After a divorce or after the kids are out of the house, we often hear women say, *I don't even know myself.* You can be a mother, wife, entrepreneur, and employee without losing your identity. The best thing you can do for yourself, your spouse, and your kids is stay true to your core. Grow, evolve, heal… just don't lose yourself; don't lose your voice."
- Mrs. Megan Allen, married since 2014

REAFFIRMING YOUR LOVE & COMMITMENT TO MARRIAGE

Why is it important to reaffirm your love? In the same way you take your car in for an oil change and a tune up, you have to service your marriage before the check engine light comes on.

There were times in my own marriage when I felt lost. Nothing major was going on, but things just felt out of sync, and I recognized that my marriage was in trouble. Going on about my day-to-day life was difficult, mainly because I honestly didn't know if my marriage was going to survive. Routine planning such as registering my son for summer camp became a burden. In the back of my mind, I was thinking I might be a single parent by the time summer rolls around. I had to weigh every decision against these two scenarios in my head. What will this look like if I'm married, but what will this look like if I'm divorced? Planning for an uncertain future was exhausting.

Likewise, men experience some of these same feelings. Maybe not to the same extent as women, but they recognize when your attention is elsewhere. You could be focused on the children, your education or on your career. Unfortunately, some husbands jump to the wrong conclusion and wonder if your heart is no longer with them. A periodic marriage tune up is a great way to check in and reassure each other that your love is still strong.

What does this look like? It can look like many different things. Early in my marriage, I found it challenging to remain tactful during times of "intense fellowship". I would yell, stonewall, and threaten to leave my husband. Later on, I found it easier to express my concerns by writing a letter. Instead of ambushing him over dinner, I would email the letter for my husband to review and then we would discuss it at a mutually agreed upon time. Your marriage tune-up could be as simple as asking your husband, are you happy? Not during times of conflict, but perhaps every few months when things are going well. This is just to ensure you both are on the same page. If your place of worship hosts an annual couple's retreat, this is also a great time to check in with each other. A few days away from the hustle and bustle of daily life is always helpful.

In nature, clouds collect water until they become too heavy, then rain falls in order to cleanse the earth. The same is true for marriage. Times of conflict occur when we've carried heavy things for too long. But if handled with grace and love, conflict can bring growth and maturity. That's why so often we look to older couples and those who have been married longer for advice. But also, during natural storms, we use an umbrella for protection. The umbrella of submission is a tool to protect and cover you from the storms of life. When you need reassurance as a wife, but your husband is not communicating or partnering with you, it's important to maintain your integrity. Submit yourself as unto God and seek wise counsel during these times.

It can be difficult to love and respect your husband during the stormy seasons of marriage. During times when you don't like each other. I know there were days when my husband didn't like me, and that's okay. At times, the feeling was mutual. But love covers all. That same respect I have at work when managers and colleagues are acting crazy; and the same love I have for my young son when he's tearing up my house. There's no reason why I can't apply this same love and respect for the man I pledged my eternal love to. Even if it requires a bit of reassurance from time to time.

RECOMMENDED BOOKS FOR FURTHER READING

Chapman, Gary. 1998, 2008. Desperate Marriages: Moving Toward Hope and Healing in Your Relationship. Chicago, IL. Northfield Publishing

Chapman, Gary. 2013. The Five love Language: The Secret to Love that Lasts. Chicago, IL. Northfield Publishing.

Hunter, Millicent. 2005. Don't Die in the Winter: Your Season is Coming. Shippensburg, PA. Treasure House

LaHaye, Tim. 1994. Spirit Controlled Temperament. Carol Stream, IL. Tyndale House Publishers

Matthews, Charita. 2022. Begin with Intention: A 21-day Gratitude Journal. Clinton, MD: Matthews Media Management

Rodsky, Eve. 2019. Fair Play: A Game-changing Solution for When You Have Too Much to Do (and More Life to Live). New York, NY: G.P. Putnam's Sons

TerKeurst, Lysa. 2022. Good Boundaries and Goodbyes: Loving Others Without Losing the Best of Who You Are. Nashville, TN: Thomas Nelson Books

Toler, Lynn. 2012. Making Marriage Work: New Rules for An Old Institution. Chicago, IL: Bolden

MARRIED BUT SINGLE

www.ingramcontent.com/pod-product-compliance
Lightning Source LLC
Chambersburg PA
CBHW020234170426
43201CB00007B/425